Light in
Watercolour

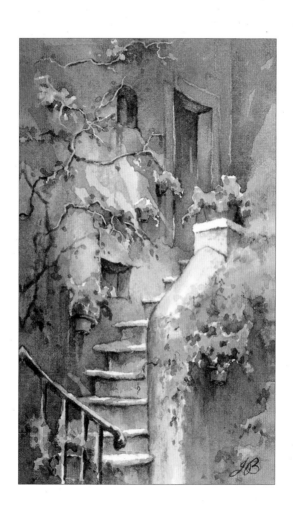

In loving memory of my dad
and with thanks to mum for her constant support
and to John, my inspiration

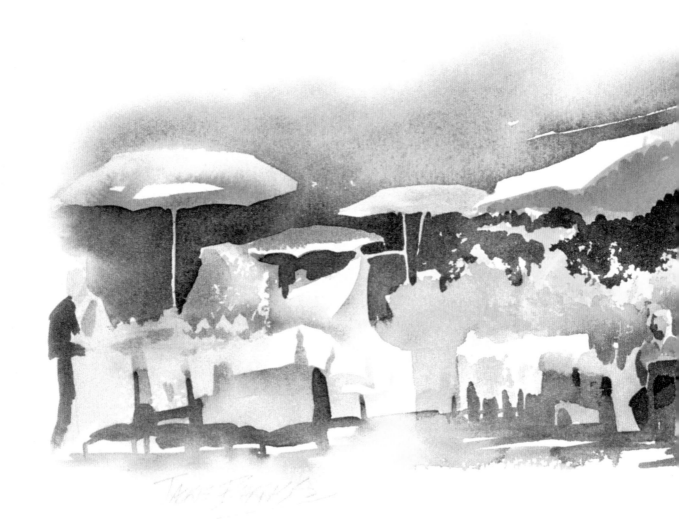

Light in Watercolour

JACKIE BARRASS

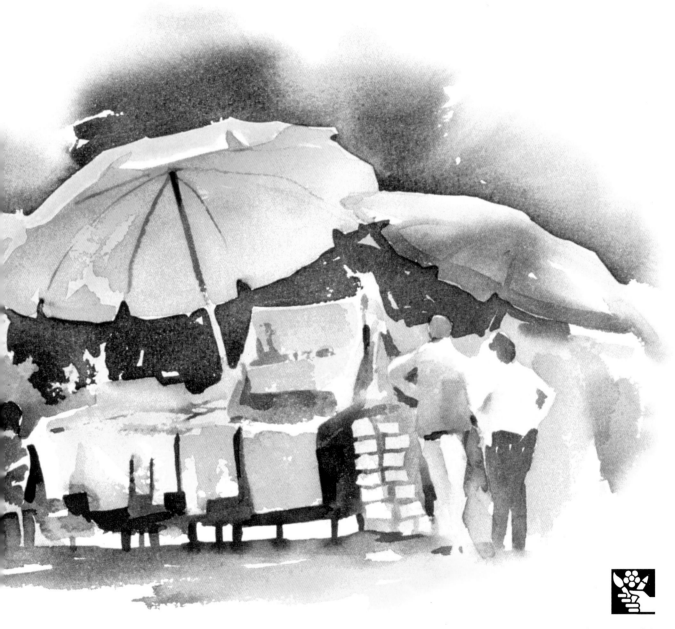

SEARCH PRESS

First published in Great Britain 2000

Search Press Limited
Wellwood, North Farm Road,
Tunbridge Wells, Kent TN2 3DR

Text copyright © Jackie Barrass 2000

Photographs by Search Press Studios
Photographs and design copyright © Search Press Ltd. 2000

ISBN 0 85532 906 8

The Publishers and author can accept no responsibility for any
consequences arising from the information, advice or instructions
given in this publication.

The Publishers would like to thank Winsor & Newton for
supplying many of the materials used in this book.

Suppliers
If you have difficulty in obtaining any of the materials and
equipment mentioned in this book, then please visit the Search
Press website for details of suppliers: www.searchpress.com

Alternatively, you can write to the Publishers at the address
above, for a current list of stockists, including firms who operate
a mail-order service, or you can write to Winsor & Newton
requesting a list of distributers.

Winsor & Newton, UK Marketing
Whitefriars Avenue, Harrow,
Middlesex, HA3 5RH

Publishers' note
All the step-by-step photographs in this book feature the
author, Jackie Barrass, demonstrating how to paint light in
watercolour. No models have been used.

Colour separation by Graphics '91 Pte Ltd, Singapore
Printed in Spain by A.G. Elkar S. Coop, 48180 Loiu (Bizkaia)

Front cover
Frosty Morning Borrowdale
360 x 305mm (14 x 12in)
*The morning sun begins to burn off the hoarfrost of autumn in
Lakeland. Masking fluid was used to retain the lit edges of the
dry stone walling and salt was used to convey the misty effect
of sunlight melting the frosty icing covering the landscape.*

Page 1
Italian Stairway
70 x 120mm (2¾ x 4¾in)
*The last rays of evening sunlight penetrate a corner of a
courtyard illuminating the staircase. Masking fluid was used
to protect the fine detail and highlights.*

Pages 2–3
Street Market
610 x 280mm (24 x 11in)
This sketch concentrates on positive and negative shapes.

Page 5
Rocking Chair
135 x 210mm (5¼ x 8¼in)
This study aims to capture light and movement.

Contents

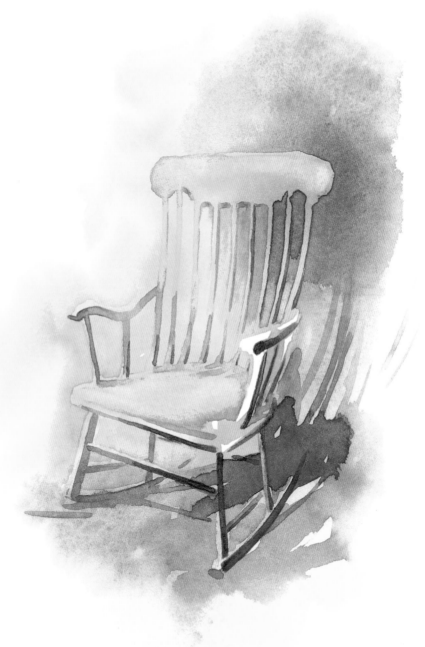

Introduction

Artists over the centuries have employed many different methods to capture light and its transient effects. The reason for this is that light has such a great impact on a painting. Often the most mundane subject matter can be transformed into a beautiful painting simply by capturing the play of light falling on it.

The glowing transparency and spontaneity of watercolour make it an ideal medium with which to interpret some of the illusive qualities of light. In addition, watercolour is well-suited to working out of doors. It is lightweight, easily transported, quick and clean to use, and unlike oils it dries almost immediately. Historically its use was restricted to sketching and preparatory work for large oil paintings, but thankfully those days have gone and watercolour is now highly regarded as a medium in its own right.

When taking your first steps with watercolours it is best to work on a small scale and to keep your subjects simple. When you have gained confidence and can manipulate the medium with greater freedom, it is then time to give more consideration to your subject matter. Until then, practise the basic washes as much as you can. Be economical and use both sides of your paper, and even if the results are unsatisfactory do not throw them away. A still life group, interior study or maybe a night scene can be worked over an uneven wash, and it is all good practice at layering colours. Keep your old work and at intervals, or when you are feeling low and frustrated with your progress, look back at your earlier attempts – I am sure you will be surprised at the improvement.

Beginners often aim to portray all the detail of a subject, but with experience you can learn to simplify a composition into basic shapes that can hold a painting together. You will also soon learn that when working in watercolour you need to think in reverse – from light to dark. It is by using the white of the paper surface that you can produce the cleanest, most sparkling watercolours. You need to determine at the outset where light is to be retained so that you can then preserve this throughout the painting process. This is the most fundamental principle of the medium and once grasped, everything else will start to become easier.

This book will help you think about and, hopefully, explore the exciting opportunities that arise when you study the use of light. My aim is to sharpen your perception and help you to organise your painting skills to produce expressive, individual watercolour paintings. Careful observation and planning are required to succeed – what may appear an effortless painting is usually the result of good forethought and organisation.

The guidance notes I have included are not hard and fast rules – use them as a starting point on your own road to discovery and you will soon 'see the light'. Experimentation is vital to improvement. I know only too well how often an adventurous approach can end in a muddy mess, but the journey will teach you a lot about the medium and its unpredictable habits. Most importantly, relax and have fun!

Opposite
Estaing
345 x 420mm (13½ x 16½in)
I visited the lovely old medieval town of Estaing whilst on holiday in South West France. I came across a boulangerie in a narrow lane, illuminated by soft, early morning sunlight and thought it made an ideal subject for a painting. The initial washes were laid down quite loosely to give an overall framework for what became a fairly detailed painting.

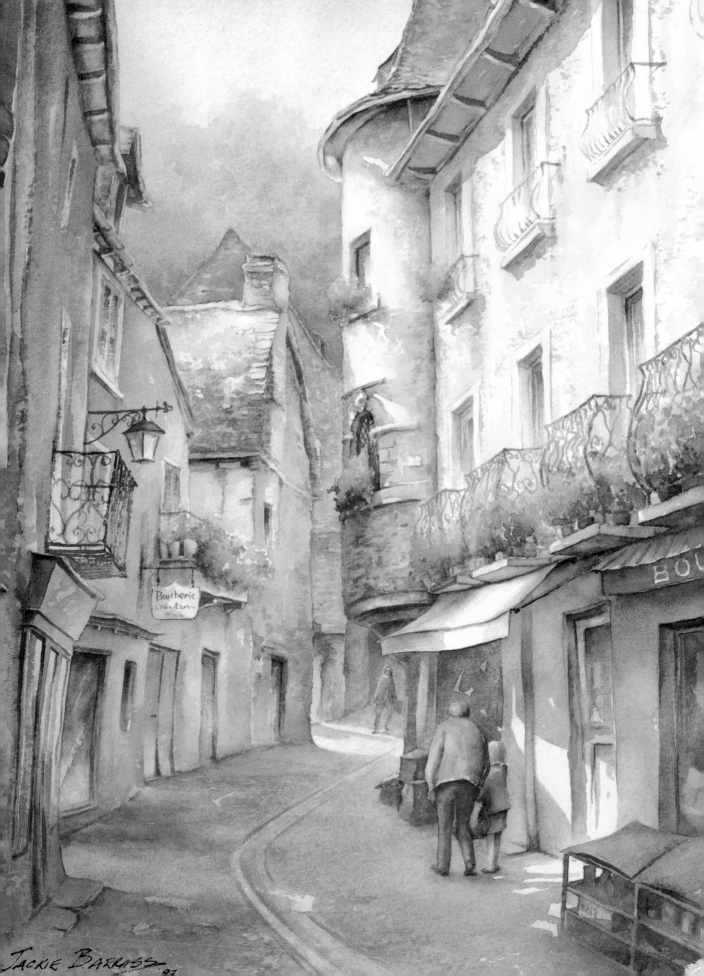

Boucherie
Charcuterie

BOU

Jackie Barrass
01

Materials

You do not need many materials for watercolour painting – in fact you can get by with just a palette and a small selection of paints, brushes and papers. Once you have found materials that you are happy with, it may feel safe and reassuring to continue using them. However, do explore other alternatives, as occasionally they can be most stimulating.

Paint

Watercolour paint is available in either pans or tubes and in two grades – students' or artists' quality. I prefer tube paint because it is ready to use, it does not require wetting and it does not wear out your brushes so quickly. Although artists' quality paint is more expensive, it produces stronger, more intense results and goes further in the long run. It is well worth the additional cost.

Palette

There are lots of different palettes for you to choose from. I use a lightweight plastic radial mixing palette. It is 305mm (12in) in diameter. It provides ample space for washes when working large areas. I also use a smaller porcelain 'chrysanthemum' palette for fine detailed work.

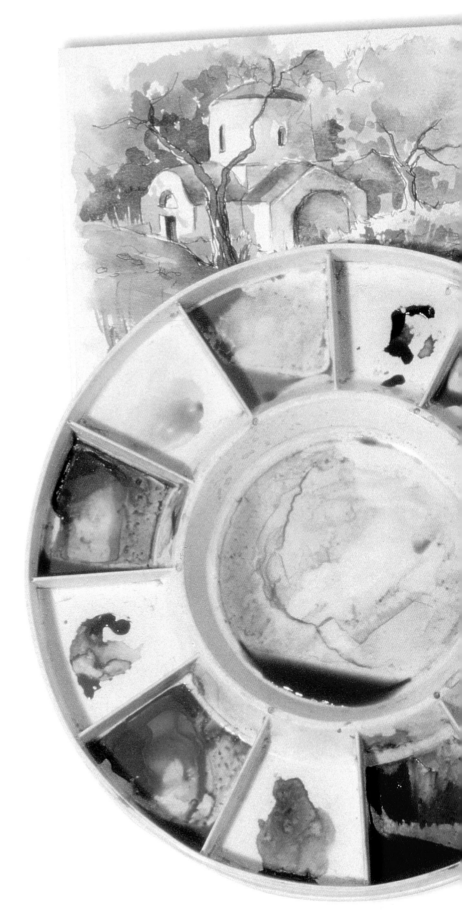

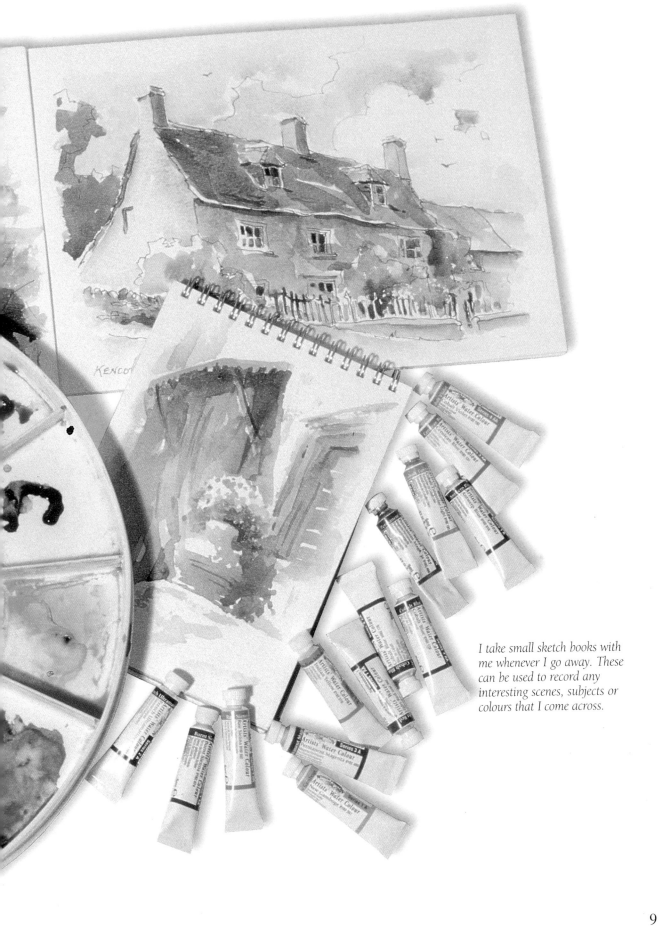

KENCOT

I take small sketch books with me whenever I go away. These can be used to record any interesting scenes, subjects or colours that I come across.

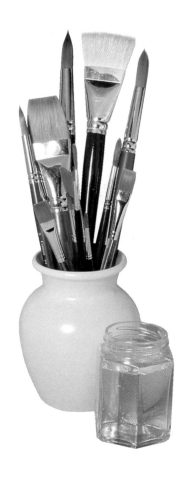

Brushes

As with paint, it is best to buy the best quality brushes that you can afford. Cheap brushes are a false economy as they wear out quickly and will impede your progress.

The most versatile brush is a **large round**. Providing it has a good point it can be used for quite detailed work as well as large washes.

A **large flat** is useful for laying down broad strokes of paint and it can also be used side-on to produce straight lines.

A **rigger** enables you to complete fine linear detail such as the delicate tracery of winter branches.

A **mop** brush is useful for softening and lifting out highlights. It can also be used to remove salt from a painting.

It is a good idea to start painting with large brushes – this will prevent your paintings from becoming fussy and overworked. The brush I use most often is a No. 14 round. This, together with a No. 6 or 8 round, a 25mm (1in) flat and a rigger are all that are needed to start you off.

Always ensure that your brushes are carefully cleaned after each painting session. You should also rinse brushes thoroughly when changing colours to keep your washes clean and vibrant. You may decide to have several brushes on the go during one painting – one for each individual colour.

Paper

Watercolour paper comes in a variety of different makes and weights. The finest-quality handmade rag papers are lovely to work on but they are very expensive and as such are impractical for beginners. Machinemade papers are excellent and widely available. They come in three textures: Hot Pressed (HP), Not or Cold Pressed (CP), and Rough.

Paper is sold and priced according to its weight. A lightweight paper will buckle when wet and this makes the paint difficult to control. It is better to use at least a 300gsm (140lb) weight paper, but even this may wrinkle if you use a lot of wet washes. Either stretch the paper before you begin (see page 14), use one of the pre-stuck 'blocks' available, or work on one of the very heavy papers, 425–640gsm (200–300lb).

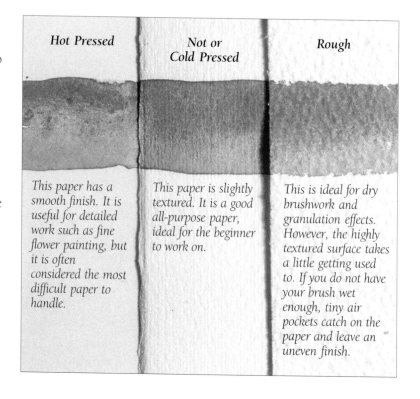

Hot Pressed	Not or Cold Pressed	Rough
This paper has a smooth finish. It is useful for detailed work such as fine flower painting, but it is often considered the most difficult paper to handle.	This paper is slightly textured. It is a good all-purpose paper, ideal for the beginner to work on.	This is ideal for dry brushwork and granulation effects. However, the highly textured surface takes a little getting used to. If you do not have your brush wet enough, tiny air pockets catch on the paper and leave an uneven finish.

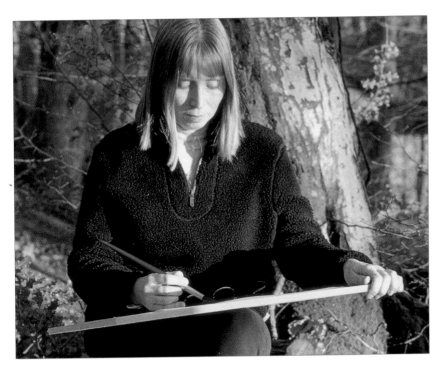

Board or easel

I work on a large architect's drawing board when painting in my studio. This can be set at any angle, from vertical to flat. However, a large rigid board (preferably plywood) is all you really need and this is what I use when working outside. Pre-stretch your paper on the board if necessary (see page 14), then prop it up to give a sloping surface while you complete your painting.

There are also a wide variety of wooden and aluminium easels available on the market, and many people find these ideal for working on. Do make sure it can be set at a suitable angle for watercolour painting before you buy one.

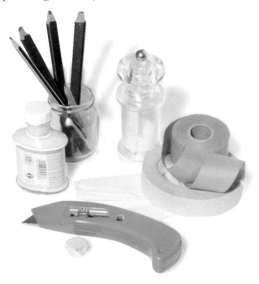

Other items

In addition to the basic materials already shown, other items that you may find useful include pencils (2B or softer) for sketching; gummed paper tape for stretching; a craft knife for removing stretched paper from a board; masking fluid and masking tape for retaining highlights and sharp edges; salt for special effects; absorbent paper for creating highlights and for general mopping up; an eraser for removing unwanted pencil marks; and a water container to keep your brushes clean and your washes bright.

Colour

Colour is light. The spectrum shows us that white light contains all colours. An object will reflect some wavelengths and absorb others – the reflected light is the local, or true colour, of that object.

It is not possible to tell if each of us sees colours the same way, so our reaction to them is unique; it may be influenced by memories that trigger an emotional response. With this in mind, it is clear that colour can be a powerful and stimulating tool for self expression.

Some painters prefer to rely on the use of tone in their paintings – colour is secondary to light and shade. Colourists, on the other hand, incorporate colour values and the interaction of colours into every stage of their painting process.

Whichever way you perceive colour in the world around you, one point that needs stressing is that the use of colours and tones must relate to those surrounding them. Therefore, try to maintain momentum over the whole painting surface, and you will achieve a sense of harmony. Do not restrict yourself by working on one area at a time.

When trying to analyse colour in your composition, it is useful to remember these characteristics.

Hue *The name of a colour – red, blue, yellow etc. – irrespective of its tone or intensity.*

Tone *The relative lightness or darkness of a colour independent of its hue. Cadmium lemon, for example, is light in tone whilst cadmium yellow is relatively dark.*

Intensity *The brightness of a colour. Some colours, such as cadmium red, are really vibrant and can dominate surrounding colours, whereas light red is an earthy duller red with less intensity. The intensity of colours can be reduced by adding, say, a complementary colour of similar tone.*

Temperature *The closeness of a colour to the warm (red/yellow) or cool (blue/green) parts of the spectrum. However, 'warm' hues can also vary in temperature. Cadmium red is considered as a warm red, while permanent rose is much cooler. Similarly, pthalo blue is relatively cooler in temperature than French ultramarine.*

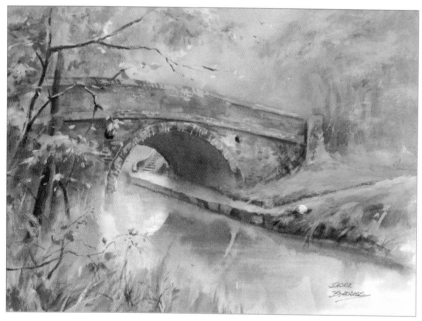

Canal Bridge
520 x 380mm (20½ x 15in)

The subtle mood of this painting is achieved by mixing colours such as the muted greys and soft pinky mauves. Intense colours would detract from this mellow composition.

You can use a limited palette of just three colours. However, although I use a large range of colours, I limit myself to a maximum of six or seven colours for any one painting. I find this helps create a sense of unity in my finished work.

Decide on your range of colours before you begin a painting. Watercolour is, of course, a fluid and spontaneous medium that does allow you some degree of manipulation as you progress, but you need a clear visual image in your mind at the outset –think about the impression you wish to convey and the colour combinations that will best achieve it.

Mixing colours

You can study the vast range of books explaining colour theory, but I believe that the only effective way to learn about colour and paint is to have a go. Whilst you can use just one of each primary colour (red, blue and yellow), I think it is best to start your palette off with two basic reds, blues and yellows (one from each end of the temperature scale) – you can mix your greens, oranges and violets (secondary colours) from these. Spend some time making your own colour wheel from the primary colours. Test the physical properties of the watercolour pigments and build up your own bank of knowledge so that using and mixing colours becomes second nature. Get to know how a small selection of pigments react with each other before introducing further colours to your palette. I suggest you avoid black, neutral tints and Payne's gray. Obtain your darks by mixing primary colours together and your paintings will have more life and luminosity.

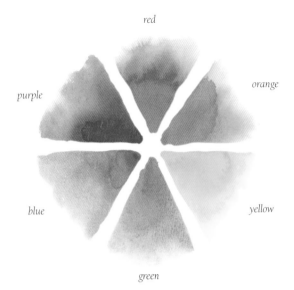

A basic colour wheel showing how primary colours (red, yellow and blue) can be mixed together to make secondary colours (orange, purple and green).

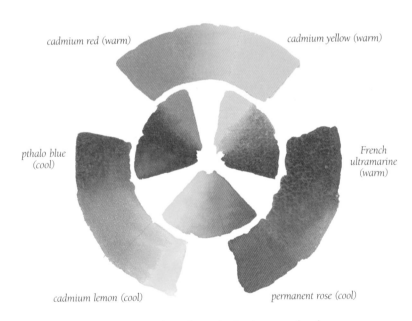

A more complex colour wheel using two of each primary colour – one warm and one cool tone. From these you can mix a large range of colours.

Stretching paper

Lighter-weight papers (see page 10) will need to be stretched before you can apply washes to them. This will prevent the paper from cockling and will give you more control when applying paint. Use gummed paper tape at least 40mm (1½in) wide and a rigid wooden board (not hardboard). The stretched paper should be left to dry flat for at least five hours or preferably overnight. Do not try to speed up the drying process by using a hairdryer as this may tear the paper or make it dry unevenly and pull away from the board.

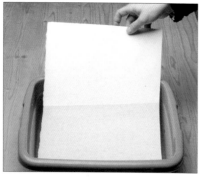

1. Soak the paper in water for a few minutes until it expands and relaxes. Shake off excess water.

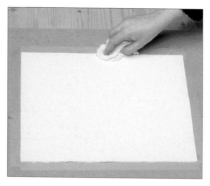

2. Lay the paper on a wooden board. Dab the edges of the paper with absorbent paper.

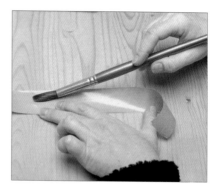

3. Dampen strips of gummed paper tape using a large paintbrush.

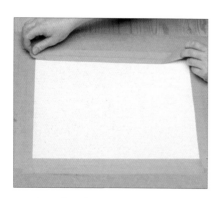

4. Use the dampened tape to attach the paper to the board. Leave it to dry flat for at least five hours.

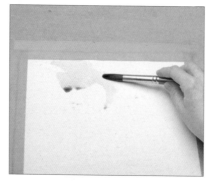

5. The paper is now ready to paint on. Do not worry if any 'cockling' occurs when you are working as the paper will tighten up again as it dries.

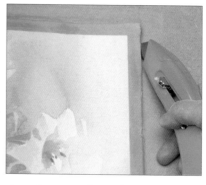

6. When you have finished your painting, cut it from the board using a craft knife.

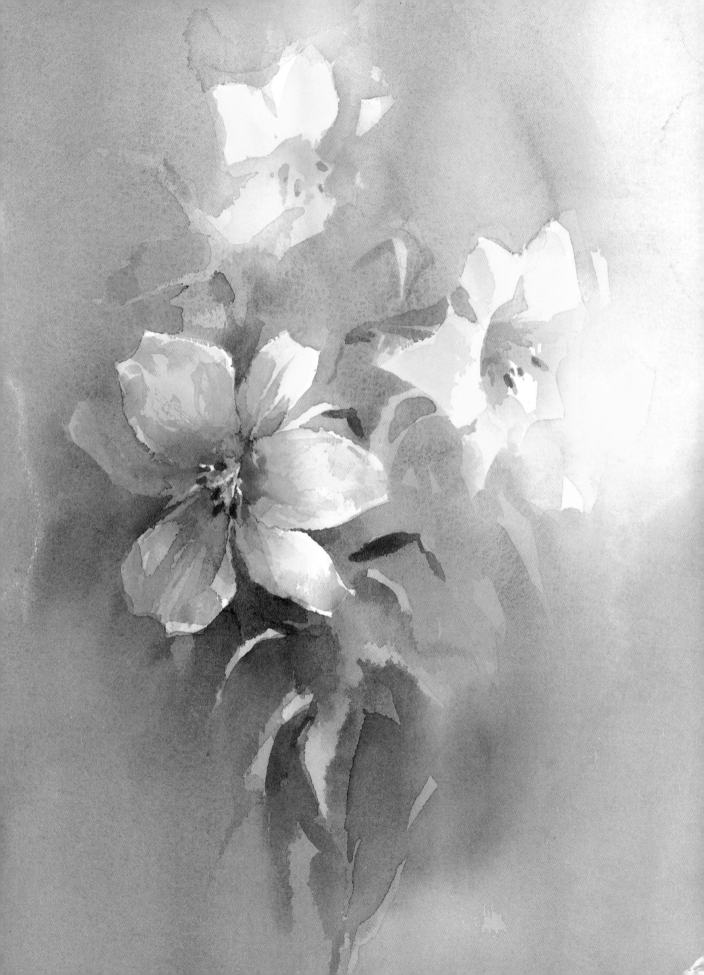

Basic Techniques

The following pages look at techniques used in watercolour painting. I have included some that are rather advanced for a beginner but I feel it is useful to show the range of 'tools' at your disposal. Concentrate on the basics until you have gained confidence. It is important that techniques are only used as aids to help you express your own ideas – do not let them take over your paintings. Suggest and simplify and let the viewer's eye complete the image. Remember that just a few brushstrokes can indicate quite detailed forms.

Washes

Washes can be flat, with one colour and tone all over, or they can be graded from dark to light by the gradual addition of water to the paint mixture. If you use two colours or more for a graded wash, it is called a variegated wash.

In each case, plenty of fluid paint must be mixed before you start as the colour needs to be applied quickly over the entire surface. Reload your brush after each stroke.

You can work onto dry paper or dampen the whole surface with water first so that the paint spreads more readily.

Your board should be tilted slightly to allow excess paint to flow down the paper or, if you are working dry, to collect at the bottom of each horizontal brushstroke and be picked up on the return journey.

Puddles collecting at the bottom of the paper should be removed with a damp brush or absorbent paper. This will prevent them from running back into the drying paint or soaking into the gummed tape and loosening your paper.

One-colour flat wash

One-colour graded wash

Wet-into-wet

Paint can be applied to a wet surface to produce a soft, diffused, ghostly effect. The wetter the paper, the less control you have. Interesting effects can be obtained working into a surface that is only slightly damp. It is a good idea to spend time testing the results that can be obtained using varying degrees of wetness.

It is probably best not to complete an entire painting with this technique, but it can be used in the initial stages and on selected areas. When combined with crisper hard-edged washes to define form, it helps to create atmosphere and unity. With practice, you can learn to judge how wet your paper is by the amount of shine on its surface.

Wet-onto-dry

Paint can be applied onto dry paper and then left to dry completely before overlaying with another colour. This gives you complete control but as a technique it is, perhaps, less exciting than wet-into-wet. I prefer to combine both methods – however, there may be times when a certain type of light, such as bright sunlight, requires just wet-onto-dry to give a crisp sparkling finish. Always think about the technique best suited to convey the mood of your subject.

Dry brushwork

This technique is perfect for creating texture and broken colour. A minimum of paint is applied to the brush and this is then dragged across the paper. The technique works best on Rough paper.

A variety of subjects from grass and foliage to rust and rock formations can be depicted by simply varying your brushstroke and brush size.

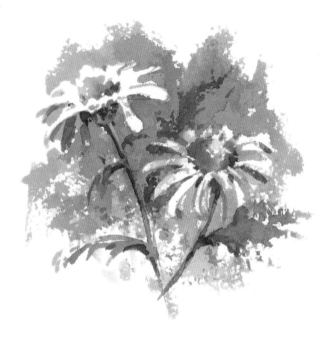

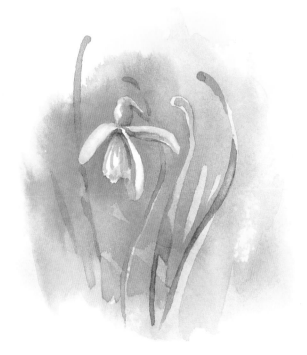

Positive and negative

This technique is also known as 'push and pull'. When painting a well-lit object you should lay down the initial wash, let it dry and then simply paint the darker area around your lit subject matter to bring it into focus. Work in reverse for dark objects seen against a well-lit background. This sounds like an obvious technique but it is often overlooked.

Softening

After carefully wetting a selected area you can use a cotton bud or soft brush to blend or merge unwanted hard-edges. Small, soft highlights can also be lifted out in this way. Be aware that certain pigments stain the paper, making it impossible to get back to a really white surface. In addition, some papers hold onto pigment more than others.

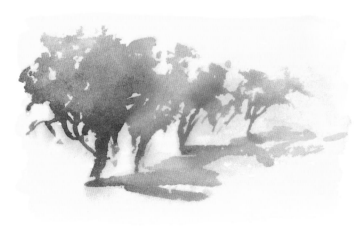

Masking fluid

Masking fluid is often frowned upon by purists but it can be very useful for protecting small details and highlights that would otherwise be impossible to retain using conventional methods. It should be used with discretion as it has a tendency to look artificial and it can stifle spontaneity. Always apply masking fluid with an old brush, and do not remove it until the paint is completely dry. Once removed, the white areas that are exposed may need to be washed with colour to suggest form and make them 'sit' correctly in the painting. Masking tape can be used in much the same way as masking fluid – for example on the straight edge of a building.

Backruns

Backruns look like accidents but they are used purposefully by many artists to great effect. Un-planned backruns can be a nuisance to a beginner and are only resolved by lifting out. They occur when fresh colour is applied to a wash before the previous layer is dry – the result is that the new paint creeps into the old. The unusual textures and edge qualities can, however, be incorporated into your painting.

Granulation

When pigment settles out of a wash into the grain of the paper it can produce lovely atmospheric speckles. This effect is known as granulation. It can add subtle interest to otherwise flat areas of paint. Certain pigments are prone to this effect (French ultramarine, for example) and some papers react better than others. Rough paper is particularly good to work on as it has an uneven surface.

Salt

Crystals of sea salt can be scattered into wet paint then left to dry to produce lovely snowflake-like shapes. This effect is caused by the salt absorbing the surrounding pigment.

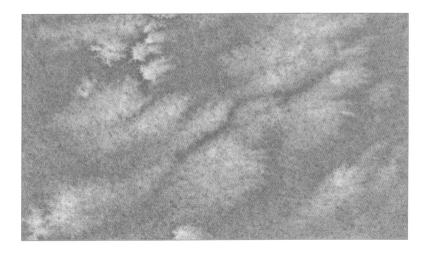

Form

Most complex three-dimensional forms can be broken down into four basic shapes: spheres, cubes, cylinders and cones. Each will have a lit side, a shadowed side and some mid tone. Light will also be reflected up from the surface plane.

In describing form, the use of hard and soft edges (sometimes referred to as 'lost and found' edges) helps to convey the character of a subject and sets up movement in a composition. Remember that our eyes do not view things with equal clarity, and light-struck edges will be sharp whilst those in shadow will be soft.

There are some 'illusions' that arise when we observe objects against light or dark backgrounds and where areas of sharp contrast meet. A dark edge adjacent to a light area will appear darker at the point where they meet, and the light area will appear lighter. Similarly, a light tone when surrounded by darks will seem lighter than that exact same tone viewed against, say, a grey background. An example in nature is the silver birch tree – here, the base will often be seen as white against the undergrowth, whereas the branches may be dark against a light sky.

Shadows intensify mood and create interest. They also anchor objects and help to clarify spatial relationships in a painting. For example, the shadow from a tree in a field shows clearly whether it is in the foreground, middle or distance. Shadows are darkest where they meet the object that is casting them, and they will vary according to the source, angle and distance of the light. Think of the late afternoon sun throwing long, distorted golden shadows across the landscape then compare these to the shadows which are cast at midday when the sun flattens the scene, or to the shadows that appear in the softer, less intense, light of morning.

When painting a still life or doing an interior study, do not rely on strip lighting as this spreads light too evenly. It is far better to use a strategically-placed lamp to add drama to the setting. Remember that light seldom falls from one single point – whether you are painting a landscape or a still life, there will be reflected surfaces within your subject and these should be full of colour and luminosity. Abstract patterns can lead the eye around a composition so plan the direction and intensity of light in your painting carefully to convey the mood you require. It is not always desirable to give a strictly pictorial rendering – if necessary change the lighting conditions to show the subject in a more dramatic, sympathetic or imaginative way.

Opposite
Water Jug and Bowl
340 x 420mm (13¼ x 16½in)
I awoke one morning to see a shaft of sunlight flooding through a gap in my curtains. It illuminated an old jug and cast a shadow of flowers on my wall. The strong contrast of light and shade clearly shows the rounded form of the jug and the highlights convey its porcelain finish.

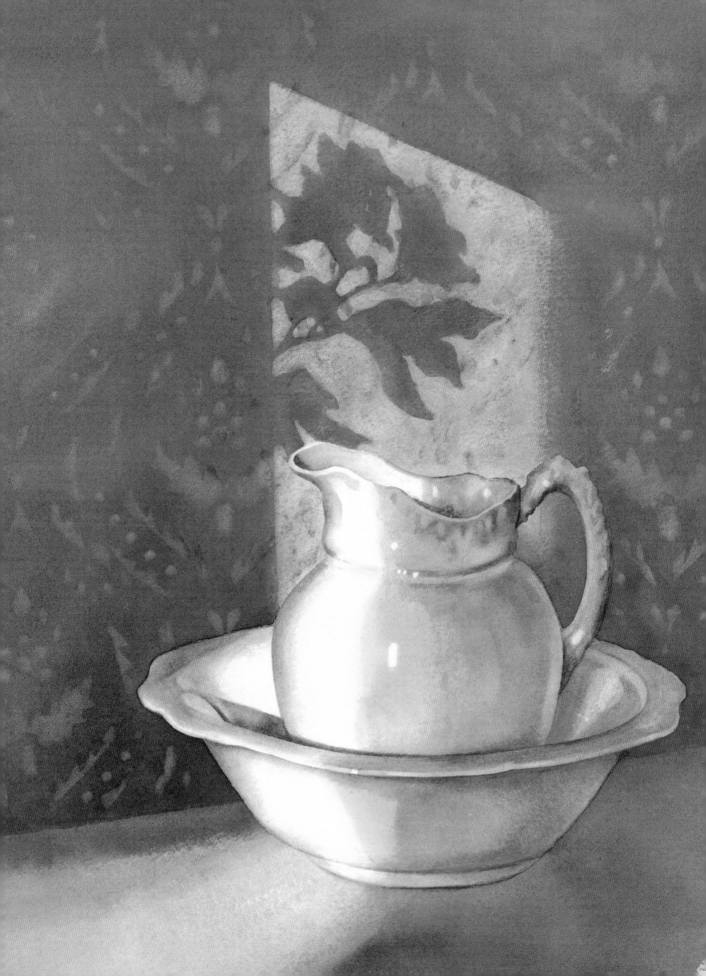

Tone

The use of tone can dramatically effect the mood of a painting. Predominant darks evoke feelings of mystery, sadness or fear. Light airy paintings are generally happy, and those which concentrate on mid tones generally produce a sense of calm and peace. Limiting tonal range has a profound effect on atmosphere, whereas a study using the full range of darks and lights is obviously lively and stimulating. All these facts need to be considered at the design stage of your painting.

When planning your painting it is very helpful to do a quick tonal sketch. This is a sort of abstract pattern or design showing lights, darks and mid tones. You need to observe the passage of light through your subject, and to contrast areas of light and dark to create depth, space and atmosphere. If necessary, turn your sketch upside down or look at it in a mirror – this will help you to forget the subject matter and concentrate solely on the design.

Tones alter when objects are seen at a distance; dark tones become lighter and light tones become darker. In other words, the tonal contrast lessens towards the horizon. Colours also become cooler at a distance. This effect is known as aerial perspective and if used it can provide feelings of depth and space.

Bear in mind that the stronger the light source is, the wider the tonal scale will be, so gauge your tones to suit the weather conditions or mood you require. For example, on a bright sunny day the full tonal range from virtually black to white is apparent; with dull conditions the range may be limited to mid-tone greys.

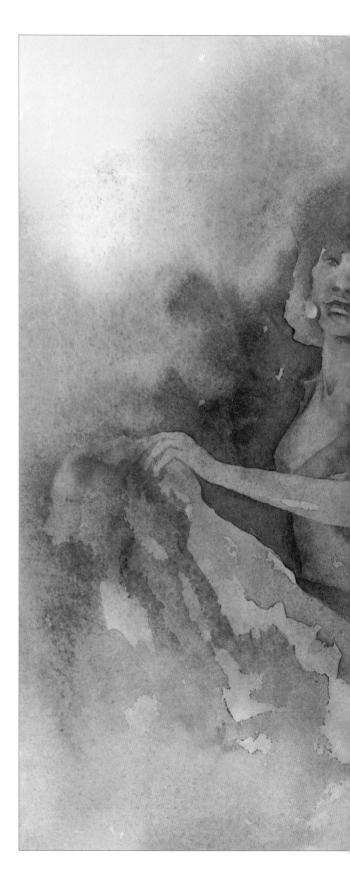

Campfire Glow
520 x 380mm (20½ x 15in)

This painting is all about atmosphere. I have tried to capture the smoky flickering light of campfires at night and the swirling movement of the dancers. The tones are dark to create a sense of mystery.

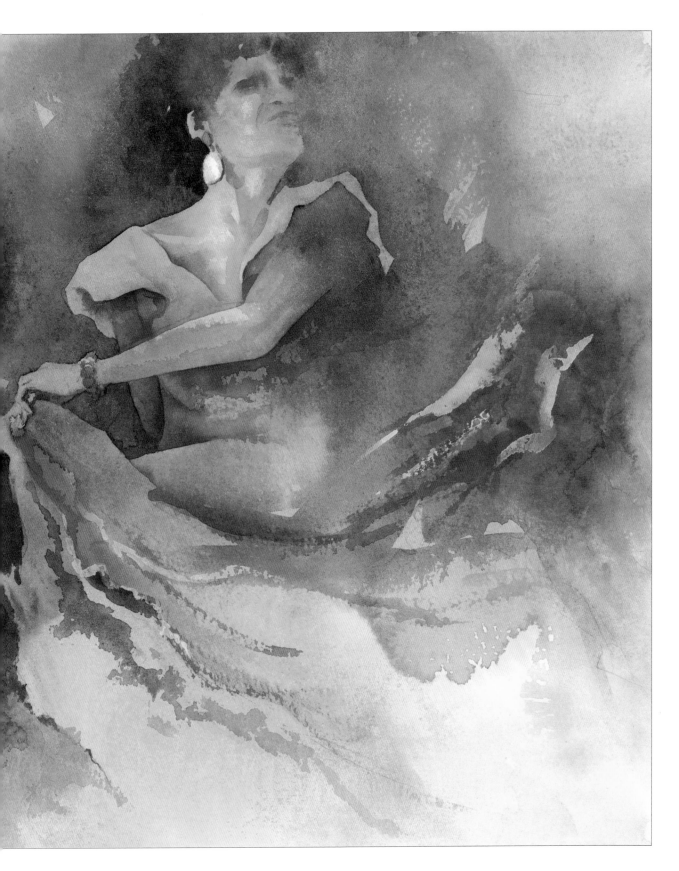

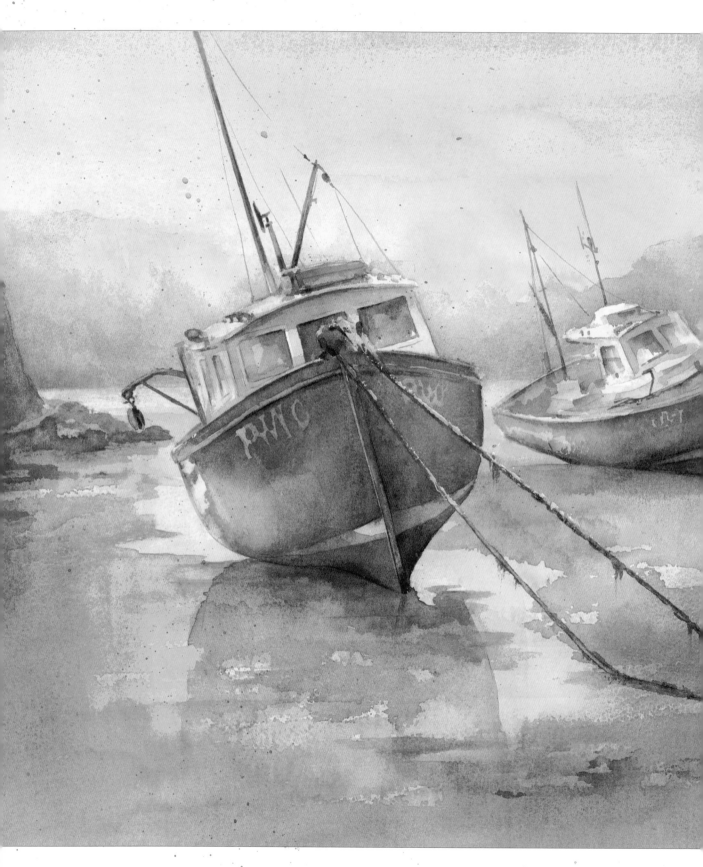

Composition

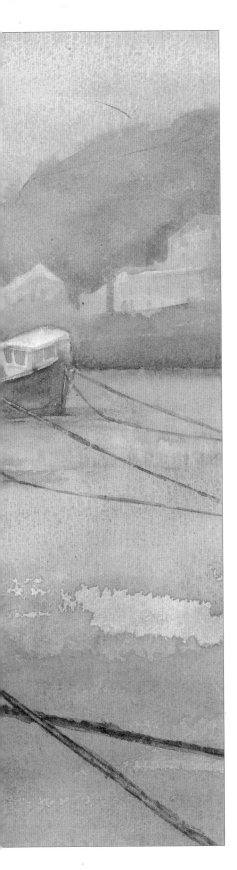

Inspiration for a painting can arise from something as simple as an interestingly shaped shaft of light and, if positioned correctly, this can be used to guide your viewer through your composition – think of a ray of sunlight coming through a window and travelling across the various objects in a room.

Whatever your subject matter you should aim to have a focal point – this is an area of interest to which the eye is drawn. If one is not obvious, then create it. Do not let your focal point become isolated, but see it in relation to the whole painting. This can be done by placing the lightest shape against the darkest to set up a visual tension, or by including a splash of bright colour, say the clothing on a figure.

Your focal point should be placed in the composition so that it retains maximum impact. To do this, divide your painting in half both vertically and horizontally to give four equal sections. Locate the focal point in one of these quarters, but not in the centre as this restricts movement, and not too near an edge as this will lead the eye out of the painting. Too much activity in the rest of your painting can be confusing so stick to your main statement and minimise detail in other areas. It helps to visualise in flat, two-dimensional shapes – looking at your scene through a viewfinder cut from a small piece of card will make this easier for you to achieve. You can 'home in' on the most pleasing view and it will also help you to identify areas of light and dark.

Finally, when thinking about the structure of your composition try to balance shapes and colours so that even if the actual features are different, the component parts are of roughly equal visual interest. If you divide your painting horizontally or vertically, then each section should be of a similar weight. For example, a large expanse of dark colour on one side can be offset by a small light area on the opposite side. Try to create enough variety to keep your viewer interested, whilst at the same time make sure that you maintain equilibrium. This can sometimes involve moving elements of your subject matter but such 'artistic licence' is allowed!

Low Tide
445 x 350mm (17½ x 13¾in)
These fishing boats were backlit by a misty sun just emerging over the distant hills – it gave a lovely golden glow to the pools of water. The ropes lead us into the composition and to the main focal point. The main mast is taken out of the picture plain breaking up the sky area, whilst the line of the hills leads us back to the focal point.

Chapel at Last Light

This simple composition will teach you to lay a graded wash, and you can also practise using masking fluid to protect highlights. Use plenty of water during the initial stage so that the whole surface remains wet. You will soon gain confidence in handling broad washes and working quickly across the entire paper surface.

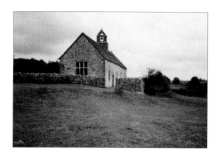

A photograph of the scene that I based my painting on.

What you need
What you need
Burnt umber, cobalt blue, cobalt violet, raw sienna, French ultramarine, permanent rose
25mm (1in) flat brush
Nos. 8 and 14 round brush
No. 1 rigger brush
2B pencil
Masking fluid
Old paintbrush, the end of a small brush or a stick
300gsm (140lb) rough paper

1. Sketch in the main components of the landscape using a 2B pencil.

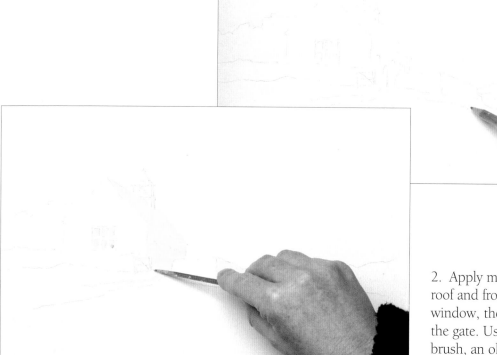

2. Apply masking fluid to the roof and front of the building, the window, the front of the wall and the gate. Use the end of a small brush, an old brush or a stick to apply it. Leave to dry.

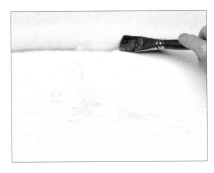

3. Mix cobalt blue with a touch of permanent rose, then use the flat brush to work a stroke of it at the top of the painting. Now work a band of raw sienna and allow the colours to blend.

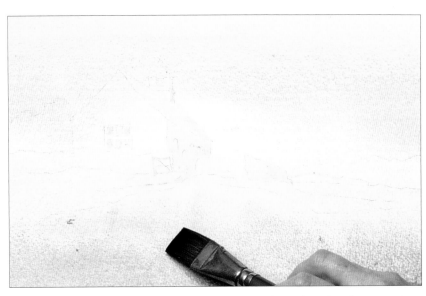

4. Continue working down the painting, applying bands of permanent rose, then cobalt violet, raw sienna, burnt umber and finally cobalt blue.

5. Use a No. 8 round brush to add touches of raw sienna here and there to introduce more light to the wash.

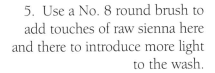

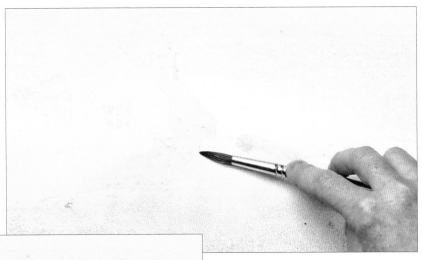

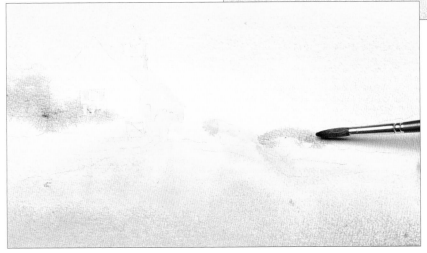

6. Build up the trees and hedges on the horizon by adding in French ultramarine.

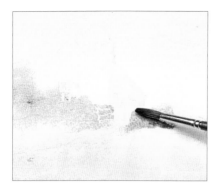

7. Add touches of French ultramarine and permanent rose to the top of the wall, then leave to dry.

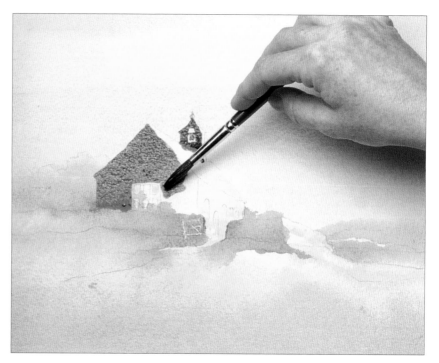

8. Paint in the bell tower and the gable end of the building using French ultramarine mixed with permanent rose. Then use the same mix to define the low wall in front of the building.

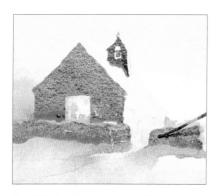

9. While the paint is still wet, use the rigger to drop in touches of burnt umber on the gable end of the building and the low wall.

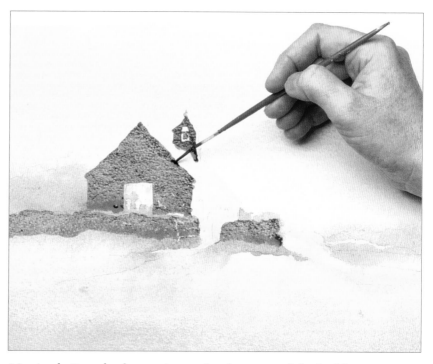

10. Apply French ultramarine under the eaves of the building. Leave to dry.

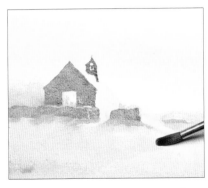

11. Use a No. 14 round brush to add a wash of permanent rose over the foreground of the painting.

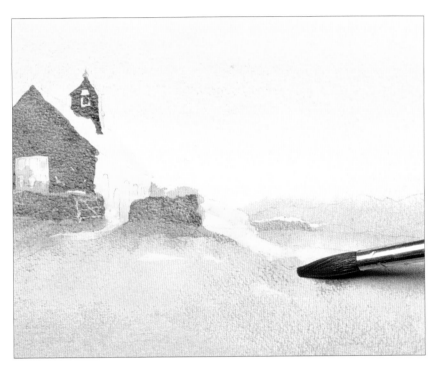

12. Complete the foreground area by adding touches of burnt umber, then leave to dry.

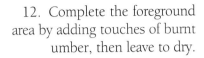

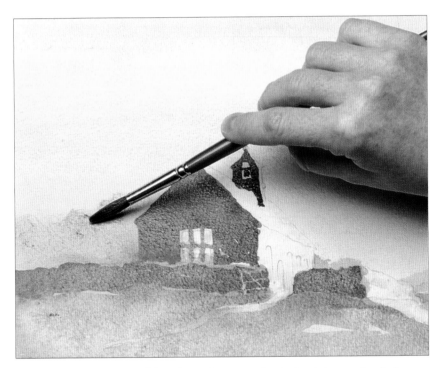

13. Use a No. 8 round brush and a mix of cobalt violet and cobalt blue to define the distant trees. Leave to dry.

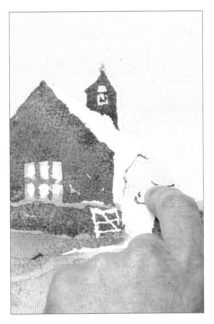

14. Remove the masking fluid.

Note *You can use a putty eraser to remove final traces of masking fluid.*

15. Use a No. 8 round brush to work a wash of raw sienna over all the areas that were masked. Strengthen the mix for the windows in the gable end of the building.

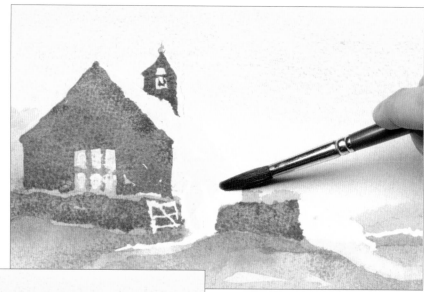

16. While the paint is still wet, add touches of permanent rose to the roof and side of the building, and to the low wall. Leave to dry.

17. Add final details to the bell tower, windows, eaves, gate and wall using a No. 1 rigger and a mix of French ultramarine and permanent rose.

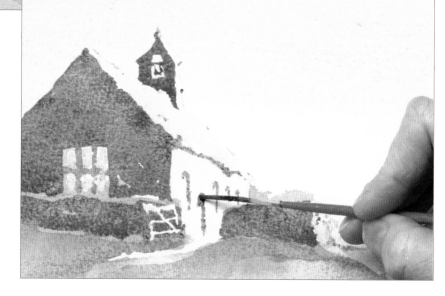

The finished painting
360 x 255mm (14 x 10in)

Light has a dramatic affect on a painting. You could add further drama to this subject by darkening the foreground or, alternatively, change the mood completely by painting the view with the sun behind you, thereby lighting the gable-end against a much darker sky.

Washday

445 x 320mm (17½ x 12½in)

This painting has a light airy feel. My attention was caught by the architectural detail of the temple shown up by the strong light. Masking fluid was used in the initial stages to preserve highlights.

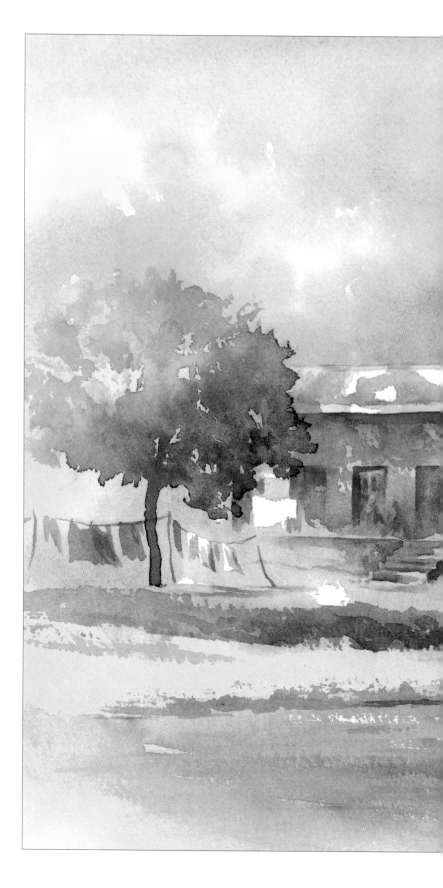

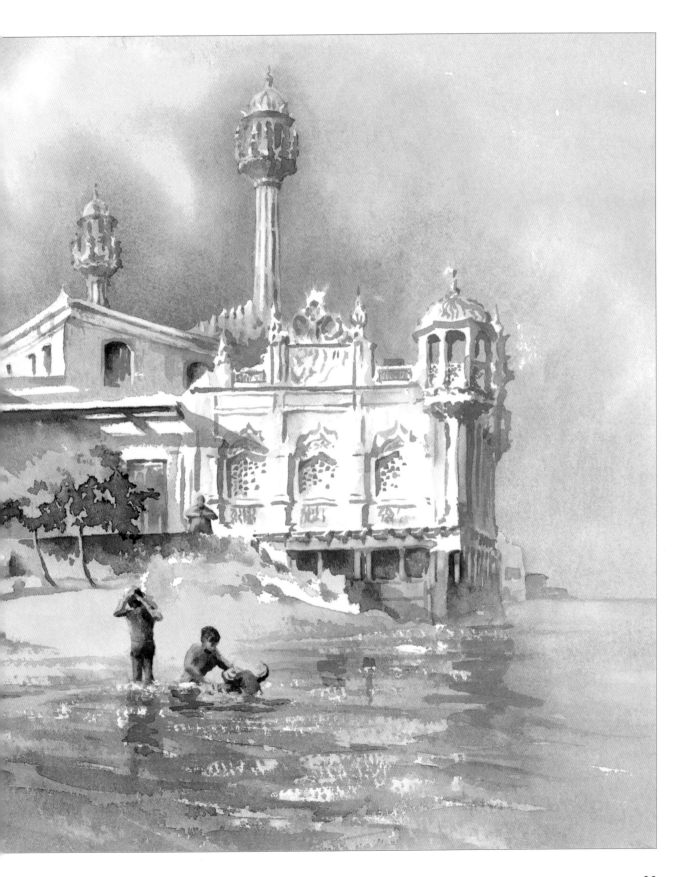

Backlit lily

Positive and negative shapes are used to portray this well-lit lily. The paint is applied using a controlled wet-into-wet technique. Let the medium do the work and try not to overpaint the flower head so that it becomes laboured and dull.

What you need

Aureolin, burnt sienna, cobalt violet, permanent magenta, pthalo blue, Winsor red

Nos. 8 and 14 round brush

No. 1 rigger

2B pencil

Masking fluid

Old paintbrush, the end of a small brush or a stick

300gsm (140lb) rough paper

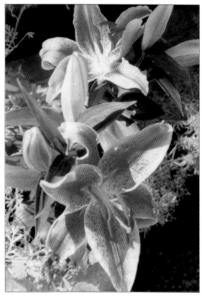

A photograph of the lilies that I based my painting on.

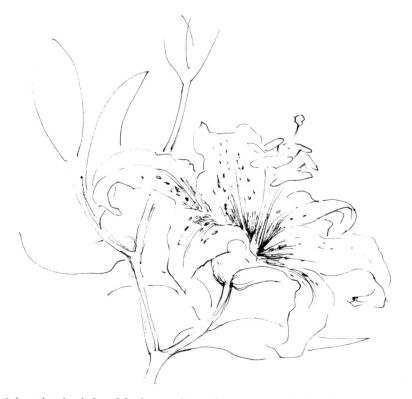

I drew this sketch from life, then used it as the composition for this demonstration.

1. Sketch in the main elements of the painting. Use the end of a paintbrush to apply masking fluid to the stamens and pistils.

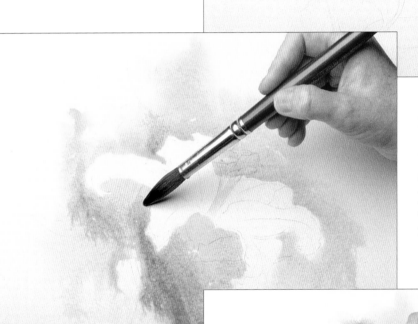

2. Roughly wet the area around the lily flower head using a No. 14 round brush. Drop in aureolin, pthalo blue and permanent magenta onto the wet areas. Allow the colours to run into each other.

3. While still wet, use a No. 8 round brush and the same colours as in the previous step to further define the edges of the petals. Leave to dry.

4. Remove some of the pencil marks around the edges of the petals then dampen the middle of the petals, leaving the very outer edges dry. Use a No. 8 round brush to drag in almost undiluted permanent magenta in the centre of each petal. This will soften off over the pre-dampened paper.

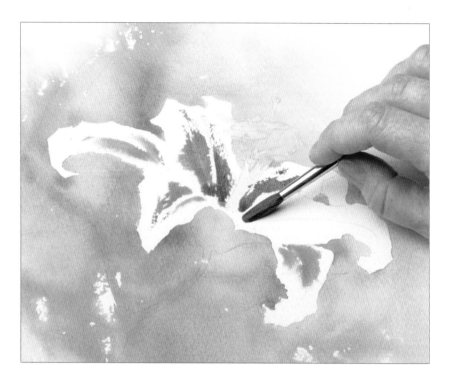

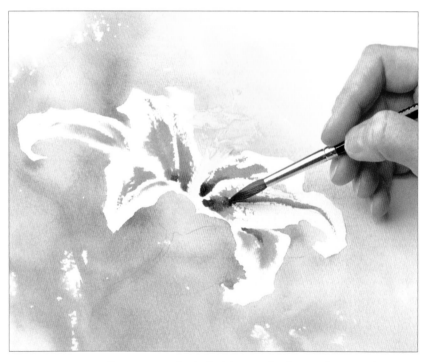

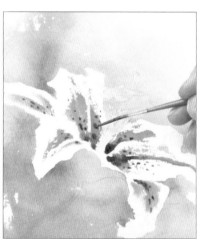

6. Use a No. 1 rigger and permanent magenta mixed with a touch of Winsor red to add spots around the base of the petals. Leave to dry.

5. Drop in a small amount of pthalo blue at the base of some of the petals to give impact.

7. Remove the masking fluid from the stamens and pistils, then paint the base of the stamens using aureolin and a No. 8 round brush. Leave to dry.

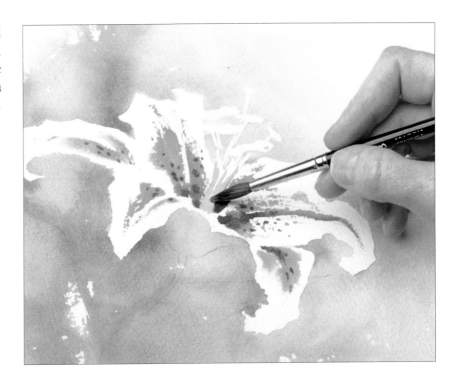

8. Paint in the pistils using burnt sienna and a No. 1 rigger brush. Leave to dry.

9. Use a No. 8 round brush and a mix of pthalo blue and burnt sienna to lightly define the stems, buds and leaves.

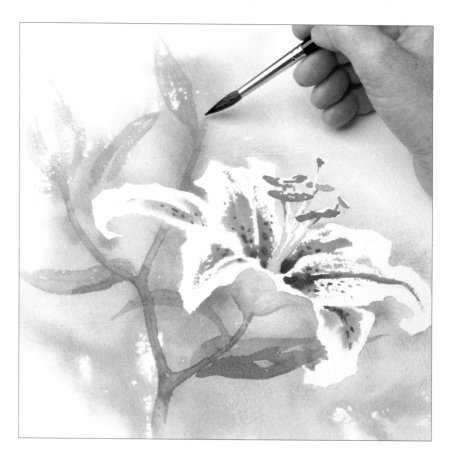

10. Use cobalt violet followed by pthalo blue to introduce shadow to the petals.

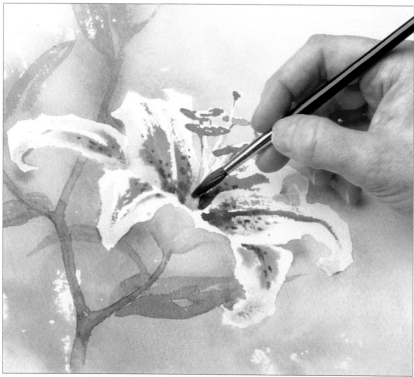

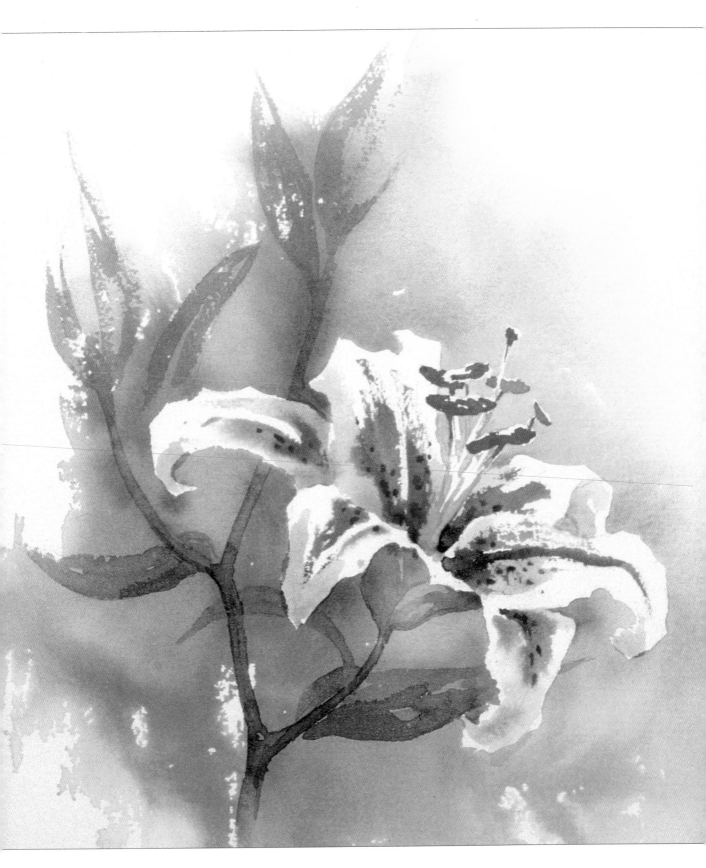

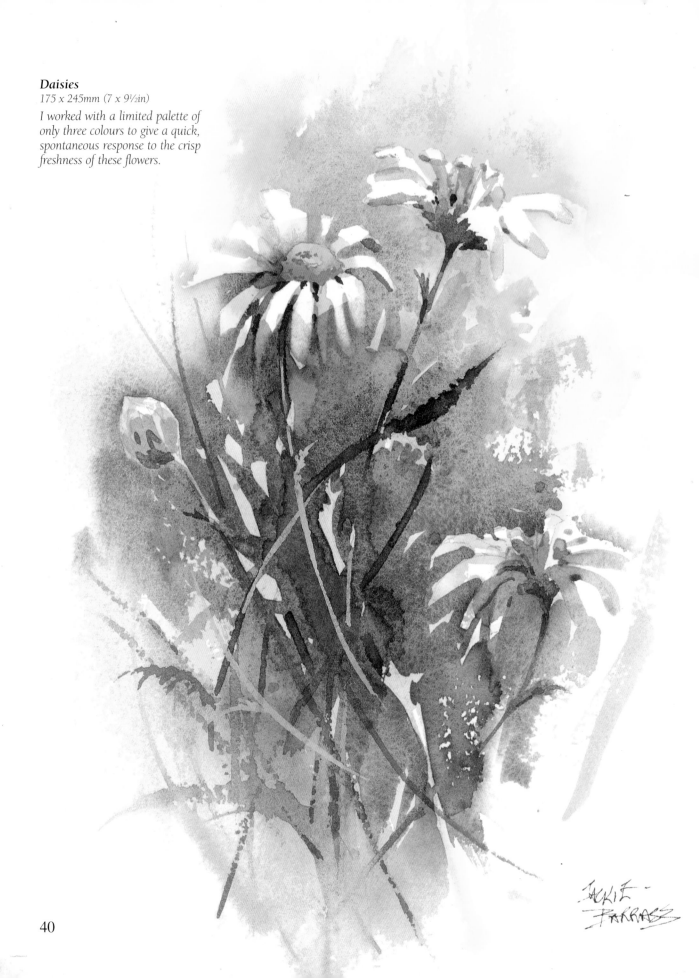

Daisies
175 x 245mm (7 x 9½in)

*I worked with a limited palette of
only three colours to give a quick,
spontaneous response to the crisp
freshness of these flowers.*

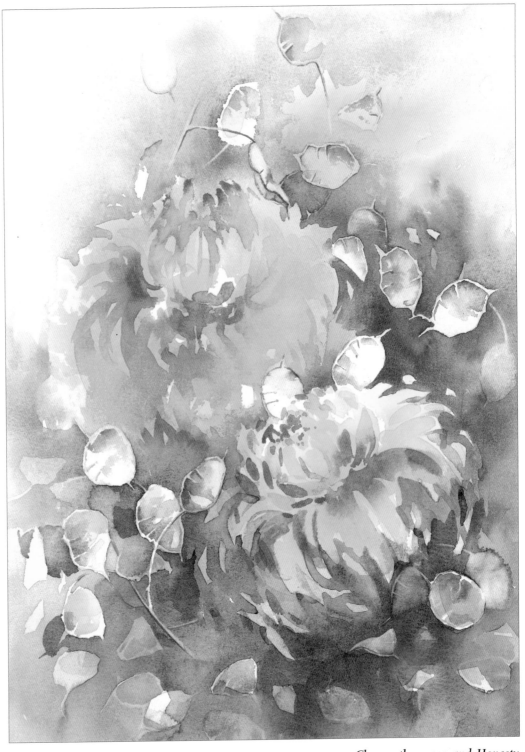

Chrysanthemums and Honesty
235 x 330mm (9¼ x 13in)

These big shaggy flower heads contrast sharply with the paper-thin seed pod linings of the Honesty to create an almost abstract design. No masking fluid was used, but some highlights were lifted out by using the softening technique.

41

Greek Stairway in Shadow

This demonstration shows how to break down a complicated subject into basic shapes and colours. It is executed in two stages, with the paint flowing over pre-dampened paper. Salt is used in this demonstration. The grains soak up the water and pigment around them to create the effect of pin pricks of light. The painting is loose and spontaneous but 'sketches' such as this can make a charming picture.

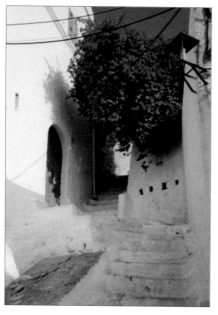

A photograph of the scene that I based my painting on.

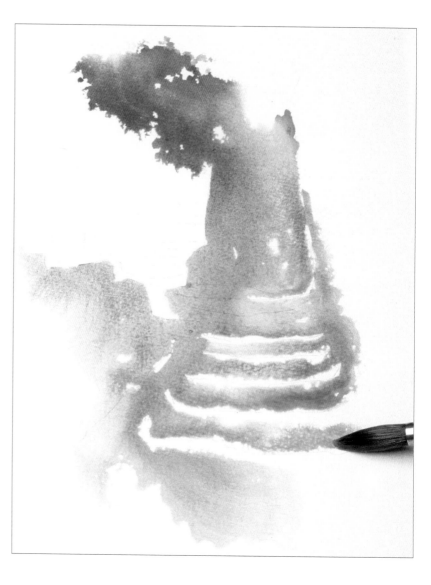

1. Sketch in the main elements of the picture. Use a No. 14 round brush to roughly wet the top left hand side of the flowering creeper, then down the steps and round into the foreground. Leave small areas on the top of the steps dry to create highlights. Drop in pthalo blue, permanent magenta, aureolin, French ultramarine and cobalt turquoise and allow the colours to blend.

42

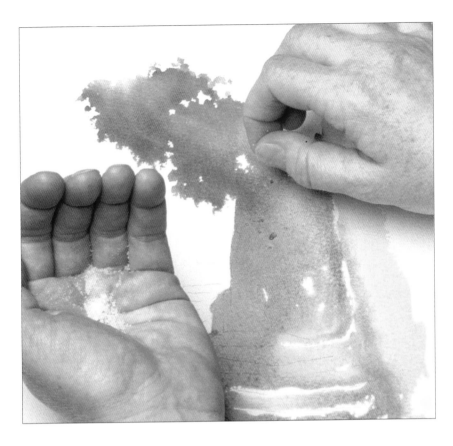

2. While still wet, sprinkle a few grains of salt in the shadowed area underneath the flowering creeper. Leave to dry thoroughly.

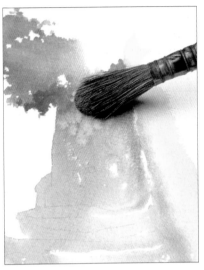

3. Use a clean dry mop brush to gently remove the salt.

4. Wet the left hand area of the painting. Use a No. 8 round brush to drop in permanent magenta, cobalt turquoise and aureolin underneath the flowering creeper and down to the top of the stairs. Leave to dry.

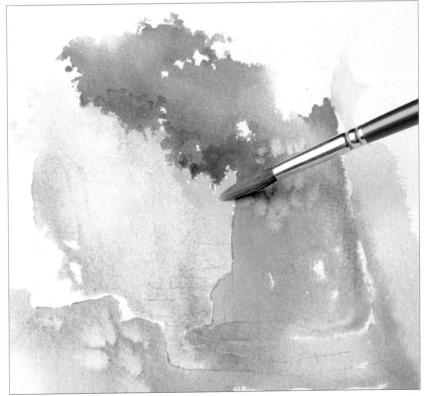

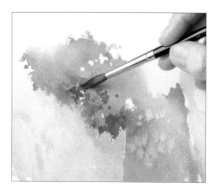

5. Use a No. 8 round brush and permanent magenta to add a little detail to the flowers.

6. Define the distant steps using a mix of French ultramarine and permanent magenta. Leave to dry.

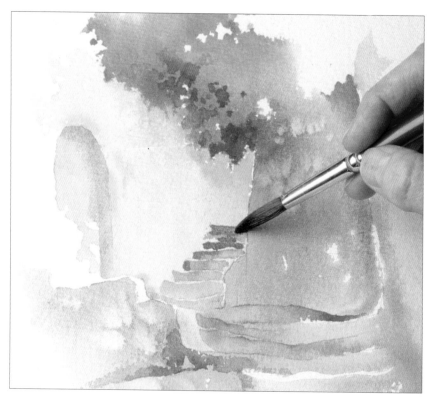

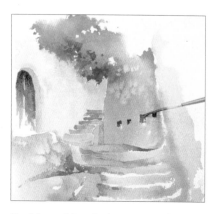

7. Use a No. 1 rigger to paint in the door and the holes in the stone wall opposite with burnt umber and pthalo blue.

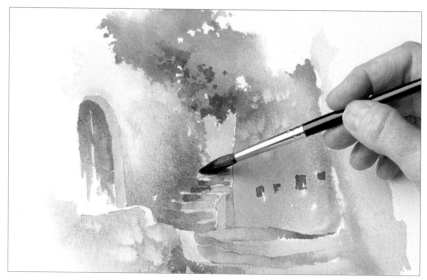

8. Add shadow to the left-hand wall using a No. 8 brush and French ultramarine mixed with a touch of permanent magenta.

Opposite
The finished painting
200 x 310mm (8 x 12¼in)
Simplification of the subject and the immediacy of the medium help to capture this typical Greek scene.

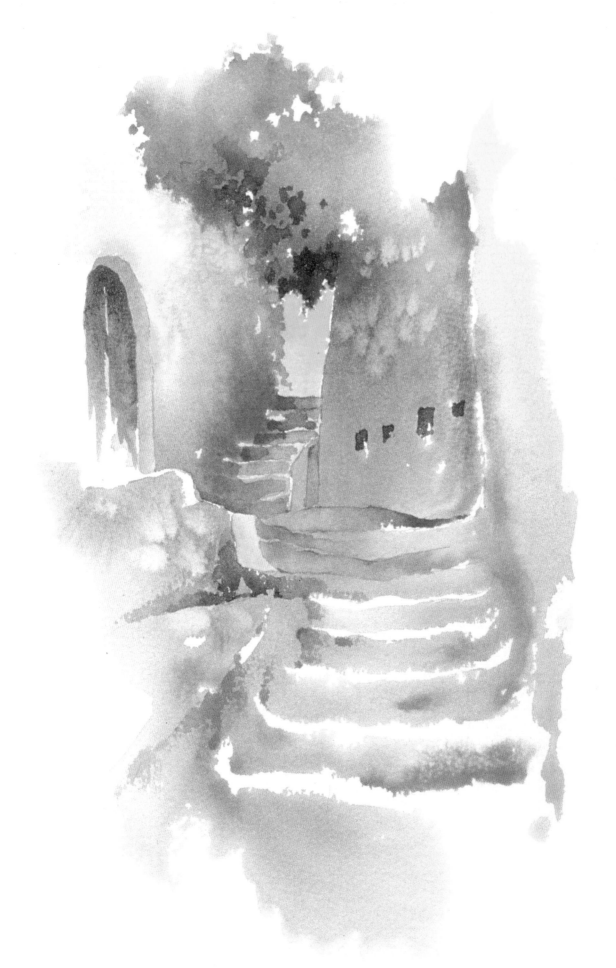

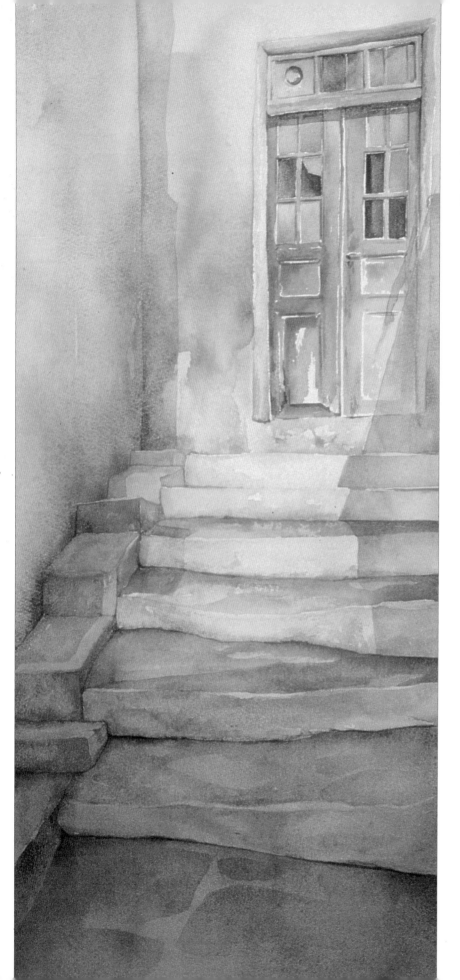

Passage of Light
280 x 610mm (11 x 24in)

The shaft of sunlight made an
interesting shape in this doorway and
set up lovely areas of reflected light in
the shadows. Darks have been
strengthened in the foreground to
give the impression of a shaded,
narrow alleyway.

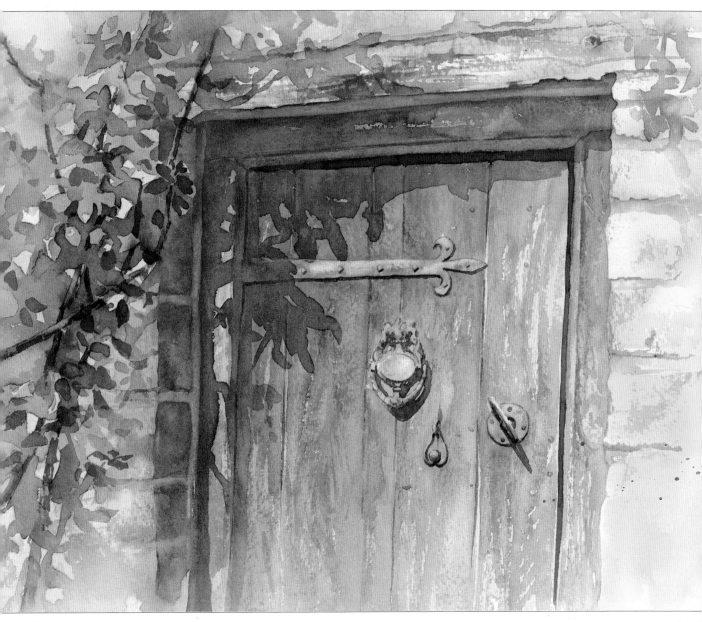

Old Oak Door
460 x 360mm (18¼ x 14in)

*Rough textured paper was used to create the appearance of
weathered wood on this door. The foliage has been treated very
simply, concentrating more on the shadows than the foliage itself.*

Index

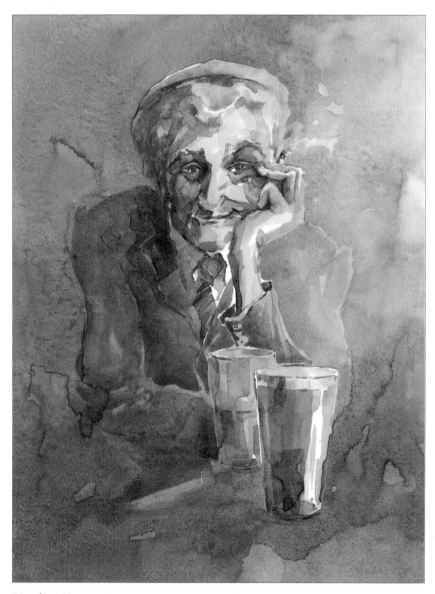

Line 'em Up
245 x 330mm (9½ x 13in)

Hot pressed paper was used for this study. The paint was applied freely, leaving
backruns to suggest the smoke-filled atmosphere of the bar.